D1562448

Living Right

Amina S. McIntyre
Music and Lyrics by Patty Mack

Living Right may be produced at churches with no royalties. Writers must be credited. Copies of the play may be made freely for this purpose.

If it is produced in a theatre, there is a charge of $25 per performance due to the writers. Copies must be purchased for each actor. Writers must be credited. Monies should be sent to:

Amina S. McIntyre
P O Box 110063
Atlanta, GA 30311
aminasmcintyre@gmail.com

Potential script alterations, outside of song selections, should be submitted to the writers for approval.

ISBN: 1535105763
ISBN-13: 978-1535105767

DEDICATION

To Westside CME Church
for making room for my gifts, no matter the idea

PRODUCTION HISTORY

Living Right was first produced at West Side Community CME Church under Rev. Reginald G. Barnes, Sr. on Sunday, April 4, 2010 under the direction of Jimmy Jucks and co-directed by Amina S. McIntyre. Lynneesse Wooten, sound and Erin Prentiss, Light Director.

The Cast included:

JOSHUA BETHELEM	Aaron Baker
SAMARRA	Amina McIntyre
AMARA, Samarra's daughter	Sydney Sommerville
MEKA, Samarra's friend	Shonda Barnes
NILON, Samarra's boyfriend	Jonathan Jucks
IAN, barber	Emmitt Starr
MARIO, Nilon's friend.	Jabari McIntyre
NEIL	Wayne Shaw
POLICE OFFICERS	Jabari McIntyre/
	Victor McIntyre
LAWYER	Inger Richardson
JUDGE	
DANCERS:	Andrea Robinson
	Amanda Barnes
	Cheean Robinson
	Chelsea Gordon
JESUS	Gary Barnes

Living Right was revived for the Connectional Youth and Young Adult Conference 2016 in Memphis, TN at the Memphis Cook Convention Center on Monday, July 11, 2016 Directed by Amina S. McIntyre. Stage Managed by Nicole Cantrell. Music and Lyrics by Patty Mack-Cole. Music directed by Arreasha Lawrence. Choreographed by Jimmy Jucks.

The Cast included:

JOSHUA BETHELEM	Josh Sole
SAMARRA	Tammy Waller
AMARA, Samarra's daughter	Bria Johnson
MEKA, Samarra's friend/CHORUS	Alecia Terry
NILON, Samarra's boyfriend	Austin Holmes
IAN, barber/POLICE OFFICER	Kevin Padilla
MARIO, Nilon's friend.	Diran Johnson
NEIL	Christopher Buie
JUDGE/SINGER	Ashdyn Unique Neal
CHORUS	Patty Mack-Cole
	Jimmy Jucks
	GaBrielle Mack
	Egypt Lawrence
DANCERS	Nyla Cantrell
JESUS	Aaron Baker
MUSICIANS	Isaiah Ellis

CAST

JOSHUA BETHELEM
SAMARRA
AMARA, Samarra's daughter
MEKA, Samarra's friend/CHORUS
NILON, Samarra's boyfriend
IAN, barber/POLICE OFFICER
MARIO, Nilon's friend.
NEIL
JUDGE/SINGER

CHORUS

DANCERS
JESUS

TIME
Today.

PLACE
A city near you.

PRODUCTION NOTES
The play was written to be used either alone or as a church service of Communion. If as Communion, add a New Testament scripture into the scene with Samarra's discussion with Meka.

*Lights up. The dancers, who are sitting in the audience, are chatting
with each other. JESUS enters, covered completely. As HE passes by
the seats, the dancers all stand and chat about the man. As the song
nears the end, JESUS and the dancers exit.*

CHOIR.
COME, COME CHILDREN COME
COME PEOPLE COME, COME
WON'T YOU COME

COME, COME CHILDREN COME
COME PEOPLE COME, COME
WON'T YOU COME

COME THEY TOLD ME
THE NEWBORN KING TO SEE
COME THEY TOLD ME
WON'T YOU COME

TODAY HE LIVES FOR YOU
ONE DAY HE'LL CRY FOR YOU
AND THEN HE'LL PAY YOUR PRICE
SO WON'T YOU COME

COME THEY TOLD ME
THE CHRIST KING TO SEE
COME THEY TOLD ME
WON'T YOU COME

TODAY HE LIVES FOR YOU
ONE DAY HE'LL DIE FOR YOU
AND THEN HE'LL RISE, YES HE'LL RISE
SO WON'T YOU COME

THEN HE'LL RISE, YES HE'LL RISE
SO WON'T YOU COME
THEN HE'LL RISE, YES HE'LL RISE

9

SO WON'T YOU COME

JOSHUA walks in the room. He is an ordinary man, with jeans, a tee-shirt, and a hat. He's not dirty, but looks worn and tired. HE stops halfway down the aisle and stops to have a seat. He takes out his canteen, turns it upside down, noting that there is no water.

SAMARRA runs by carrying a large bottle of water.

JOSHUA. Excuse me, may I have some water.

SAMARRA keeps running.

JOSHUA. Excuse me, ma'am.

SAMARRA.*(stopping)* I ain't got no money for you.

JOSHUA. I don't want your money.

SAMARRA keeps running. JOSHUA throws the canteen at her.

SAMARRA. I already have a man.

JOSHUA. 3 baby fathers, 2 ex-husbands, and 1 guy you currently live with. I'd say you have many men.

SAMARRA. Who told you that? This better not be a reality TV show.

JOSHUA. No.

SAMARRA. Who are you?

JOSHUA.*(picks up canteen)* I'll be moving on now.

SAMARRA. Didn't you want some water?

JOSHUA. The water I have access to is eternal. If you'd like, you can try some from my parents.

SAMARRA. How do I know you aren't trying to trick me?

JOSHUA. You seem to be one who can see the authentic. You can tell if I'm the truth.

SAMARRA. *(sizes him up)* About this water…

JOSHUA. Pray with me.

SAMARRA and JOSHUA kneel to pray. LEADER goes to the podium.

JUDGE. *(Words are projected on screen.)* Let us unite in the historic confession of the Christian faith.

I believe in God, the Father Almighty, Maker of heaven and earth; and in Jesus Christ, His only Son our Lord; who was conceived by the Holy Spirit, born of the Virgin Mary, suffered under Pontius Pilate, was crucified, dead, and buried; the third day He rose from the dead; He ascended into heaven, and sitteth at the right hand of God the Father Almighty; from thence He shall come to judge the quick and the dead. I believe in the Holy Spirit; the Holy Spirit; the holy catholic Church; the communion of saints; the forgiveness of sins, the resurrection of the body, and the life everlasting. Amen.

JUDGE steps down. JOSHUA and SAMARRA get up and hug.

JOSHUA. Now go. Live that life no more.

The choir reprises "Come People". Lights down. Lights up on the barbershop. NEIL is in the chair, and being shaped up by IAN.

MARIO. Neil, I'll pay you back soon.

NEIL. You keep saying that but I don't see any progress.

IAN. Maybe you should give it to him as a gift.

NEIL. This is between Mario and I, foreign man, just handle your business.

NILON enters.

IAN. Salaam Aleichem.

NILON greets MARIO with a handshake.

NEIL. What up, man?

NILON. I'm alright, just a little confused.

MARIO. Man, if I had the woman you got, I'd never wonder.

NEIL. She's so sexy to be a mother. If her body was a road map, I'd read her atlas.

The men laugh.

IAN. Let's remember to respect our queens. What's going on?

NILON. That's just it. She told me today that we're done.

NEIL. Women are all the same.

MARIO. Samarra's a good woman. What happened?

NILON. She said some guy gave her some water that

changed her life.

NEIL. See, that's what I'm talking about. Probably moving in with the guy.

NILON. She's getting her own place. Something about following a new path.

NEIL. Please, you have a better chance of walking on water than that happening.

MARIO. Samarra's just sipping some of that alkaline water. You know, it makes you tingle inside.

NILON. I don't know.

IAN. She got faith, like what Jesus was trying to get Peter to understand.

NILON. I know this story.

NEIL. Then preach to me.

NILON. *(mimicking a preacher's whoop)* You see, on a particular day, after feeding the five thousand, the disciples were hanging out at see.

NILON is pretending to preach, with all the movements and the others in the shop, except IAN, become his congregation with "Amens" and such.

NILON. He sent the multitude away, and went up to the mountain to pray. You got the disciples in the middle of the sea, but Jesus is up their praying. In the middle of the night, he comes down the mountain and decides to go to the boat. The boat was in the middle of the water, not near the mountain. So Jesus decides to walk on the water to the boat.

I believe he scared the mess out of those disciples.

MARIO. *(mimicking Nilon)* I'd be like Peter. Hey Jesus, if that's you, let me come to you.

NILON. Then boy, come on.

MARIO. *(walking toward NILON)* I'm walking on water.

NILON. Yea, come on.

MARIO. I'm walking on water!

NILON. Come on!

MARIO. Jesus, the wind is high, it's water!

NILON. Just walk.

MARIO. Save me, I'm sinking! Lawd, don't let me drown.

NILON. Oh ye of little faith.

The room starts laughing, all but IAN.

IAN. Joke if you want to my friends. Fact is, your bible says that it is a lesson in faith.

JOSHUA walks past the door. The guys look at him.

NEIL. Fact of the matter is, some man convinced your woman to leave you. After all you done for her. Does make your mind wonder.

IAN. Who else but God can do that?

Lights down on the barbershop. Music for "Jesus the Way" cues.

14

CHOIR.
VERSE: WHEN YOU'RE IN NEED OF SHELTER
AND YOU'RE LOST AND ALL ALONE
IF YOU'RE LOOKING FOR A SAFE PLACE
AND YOU CAN'T FIND YOUR WAY HOME
I KNOW THE WAY...THE WAY TO GO
I KNOW THE WAY...THE WAY TO GO

IF YOU NEED A SHOULDER TO CRY ON
WHEN TROUBLE TAKES ITS TOLL
IF YOU NEED A FRIEND TO RELY ON
WHO WILL COME AND CALM   THE STORM
I KNOW THE WAY...THE WAY TO GO
I KNOW THE WAY...THE WAY TO GO

CHORUS
I KNOW THE WAY TO GO
DO YOU KNOW THE WAY TO GO
I KNOW THE WAY TO GO
DO YOU KNOW THE WAY TO GO
I KNOW THE WAY TO GO
DO YOU KNOW THE WAY TO GO
I KNOW THE WAY TO GO
JESUS IS THE WAY
JESUS, JESUS IS THE WAY
JESUS IS THE WAY
JESUS, JESUS IS THE WAY
JESUS IS THE WAY
JESUS, JESUS IS THE WAY

During the song, JESUS praying on the boat while the disciples look on. JESUS finishes his prayer and looks at the disciples. HE walks on the water; the disciples get scared. PETER looks over the boat's side, recognizes JESUS and waves. JESUS motions for him to come. PETER goes over the boat side, and the disciples look on as if he is crazy. PETER walks to JESUS, then looks down. HE falls on his knees and flails like he is drowning. JESUS shakes his hand, then pulls PETER up by his collar. They both get back in the boat.

Lights crossfade to AMARA and LEAH, who are giggling playing.

BOTH. (*Sing Songy, Children Chant*)
JIG A LOW
JIG JIG A LOW
JIG A LOW
JIG JIG A LOW

LEAH. HEY AMARA

AMARA. WHAT?

LEAH. ARE YOU READY?

AMARA. FOR WHAT?

LEAH. TO JIG.

AMARA. JIG WHAT?

LEAH. JIG A LOW

AMARA. WELL, MY HANDS UP HIGH,
MY FEET DOWN LOW
AND THIS THE WAY I JIG A LOW.

AMARA does a ballerina's pirouette.

LEAH. You're supposed to do something like this.

LEAH does the latest popular dance, like the Nae Nae and dab.

AMARA. You said how I jigalow. This the way I jigalow.

LEAH. I bet you make straight As, too.

AMARA. Don't you?

AMARA coughs.

LEAH. Ewww, You got the Zika.

AMARA. No, I don't! You must have it, you know what it is!

LEAH. Na uhn.

JOSHIA. We all have many gifts, but we are one body.

LEAH. Says who?

JOSHUA. Says my parents.

AMARA. I don't always believe my parents.

JOSHUA. You won't always.

LEAH. Un uhn. Ima always believe my parents.

JOSHUA. Wouldn't you work a little harder in school if you believed in them?

AMARA. We were taught not to speak to strangers.

LEAH. Yea, we should go.

JOSHUA sits by a tree.

JOSHUA. Let's talk about talents.

LEAH. We shouldn't.

AMARA. I want to.

LEAH. What if we get in trouble? My brother, Neil would be upset…

AMARA. We can't if there are two of us staying.

LEAH. Okay. But only for a few…

THEY sit near Joshua.

Lights crossfade to a living room area. MEKA is gathering furniture. SAMARRA enters.

MEKA. Hey girl.

SAMARRA. Hey. *(they hug)* So good to see you.

MEKA. For real! Spill the tea. I want to know what happened. You're moving out?

SAMARRA. Yea.

MEKA. So you quit your job and you and Nilon are broken up?

SAMARRA. Yes…That's what it seems like.

MEKA. Did you think about the kids and how this would affect them?

SAMARRA. They'll move with me.

MEKA. Nilon is a good man though, and not just because he has his own business.

SAMARRA. He's different from my husbands.

MEKA. Tyler used to pimp you. Still don't know which kids are his?

SAMARRA. I know. The man today confirmed what I thought. Tyler wasn't able to have children.

MEKA. I'm just happy to see he's gone. Amara's father, Shawn, wasn't any better.

SAMARRA. He had those good drugs though.

MEKA. I remember. When I first got sick and didn't have insurance, he got me my morphine.

SAMARRA. You still bleeding?

SAMARRA tries to hand MEKA some pills from out of a drawer. MEKA refuses.

MEKA. For twelve years. Matter of fact, it started when you went into labor with Amara.

SAMARRA. The doctors?

SAMARRA insists on handing MEKA the pills. MEKA takes them and hides them under the pillow.

MEKA. Can't do nothing. Have no clue what's making me bleed. But enough about me. Nilon is a good man.

SAMARRA. But I can't have a man who's just going to shack up with me. I need a commitment from him.

MEKA. He treats your children like his own.

SAMARRA. I know, but we have to do things right. I don't know what "right" is, but I have to try. I told the man the other day that I would sin no more. I'm keeping my promise. I already found an apartment. If Nilon loves me, he'll understand.

MEKA. Let's hope so.

SAMARRA. Let's me share something with you. From the New Testament. *(*Communion Scripture may be added here)*

SAMARRA goes to pick up her Bible. MEKA follows, but something catches her eye out the window. JOSHUA is sitting in front of LEAH and AMARA and a group of children.

MEKA. Girl, look at this.

SAMARRA. What?

MEKA. There's a man out there talking to the children.

SAMARRA looks out the window.

SAMARRA. That's Joshua, the man I met while walking.

MEKA. Girls, he's fine! I'da left Nilon too.

SAMARRA. I'm telling you, it's not like that. He's different. I'll introduce him to you.

Lights down on MEKA and SAMARRA. Focus on JOSHUA and the kids, telling stories to the children.

JOSHUA. You all should be careful to use all your talents, and be working to do right.

LEAH. But my momma said we got time left.

JOSHUA. You don't always know that. Let me tell you a

story. Once a traveler was along his way and had become very hungry. He passed by a fig tree that was full of leaves, but had no fruit. He was so angry that he cursed the tree so that he would never grow any.

AMARA. *(coughing)* But why did it go away so quickly?

JOSHUA. We all have potential, but we must have faith to make them real. Once you loose faith, you destroy yourself. Don't leave your potential, even as children, to waste away.

NEIL. *(entering)* Leah, what are you doing here?

LEAH. I just wanted to.

NEIL. All of you go inside.

JOSHUA. There is really no bother. Children learn quickly. Adults should copy their demeanor.

NEIL. What are you, some pervert?

JOSHUA. I'm just passing through.

NEIL. We don't want you messing with our children. *(taking LEAH by the arm)* Come on.

THEY exit.

AMARA. *(coughing)* Mr. Joshua, thank you for the story.

JOSHUA. You're welcome. Take care of yourself, Amara.

AMARA. I will.

SHE leaves. IAN comes from behind JOSHUA.

IAN. I appreciated your story. Please take time with me.

JOSHUA. My stories are only for Christians.

IAN. What you have is something that should be shared with many.

JOSHUA. I won't take food from the children to give it to the dogs.

IAN. But even the dogs eat the crumbs that fall from the master's table.

JOSHUA. You are well read.

IAN. In some areas.

JOSHUA. Your faith has rewarded you. Kneel with me.

JOSHUA and IAN kneel. The LEADER comes up to the podium.

JUDGE Let us pray the Prayer of Confession.

(words are projected on screen)

Almighty God, Father of our Lord, Jesus Christ, Maker of all things, Judge of all people, we acknowledge and bewail our manifold sins and wickedness, which we from time to time most grievously have committed, by thought, word and deed, against Thy Divine Majesty, provoking most justly Thy wrath and indignation against us. We do earnestly repent and are heartily sorry for these our misdoings; the remembrance of them is grievous unto us. Have mercy upon us, have mercy upon us, most merciful Father; for Thy Son our Lord Jesus Christ's sake, forgive us all that is past, and grant that we may hereafter serve and please Thee in newness of life, to the honor and glory of Thy name, through Jesus Christ our Lord.

Amen.

They stand. Joshua turns to leave. IAN stops him.

IAN. I did not come here for myself. I came for my friend, Mario.

JOSHUA stops him, looks around, then motions for IAN to come with him.

Blue light up on NEIL talking to MARIO.

NEIL. We have to get rid of him. The entire town is going to follow this man.

MARIO. I like him.

NEIL. Don't you have a debt to pay?

MARIO. Yea.

NEIL. As long as you still owe me money, you will like what I like when I say you like it.

MARIO. This is wrong. I need to go to the office.

NEIL. Did you forget about the school loan? You wouldn't be a lawyer if it wasn't for me, your benefactor.

MARIO. I'm a member of the bar, I will not violate that –

NEIL. What I'm asking is for you to take care of your community. Who lives in truth?

MARIO. I do.

NEIL. No one like this change – we have a status quo to

maintain.

MARIO. Even if it's wrong.

NEIL. We can't be wrong if we made the law. Now, what I need you to do …

NEIL tells the plan to MARIO, who doesn't seem interested. Lights down.

SAMARRA and MEKA arrive in the garden where Jesus was, but it's too late.

SAMARRA. *(looking around)* I don't see him. He must have left. I'm sorry, girl.

MEKA. It's okay.

SAMARRA. I need to get back to packing. See you later.

They embrace. SAMARRA leaves.

MEKA. Will I never find relief? It's like a storm is always brewing inside me.

MEKA sings "Peace Be Still".

A storm is brewing in the background and the dancers are on little boats. On one, JESUS, is sleeping. There as the storm gets larger, one wakes up JESUS. He stretches, and looks at the storm. He waves his hand and the storm stops. HE looks at the disciples, and then goes back to sleep. Lights down.

Lights up on NILON and SAMARRA, who is packing.

NILON. Mar, I respect your decision, but you didn't think this through. I just don't understand how a guy you met for only a second could change you.

SAMARRA. He showed me my life. I have to change how we do things.

NILON. But do you have to move out?

SAMMARA. If you love me, then you have to see how this will change my life. Besides, I want Amara to be around the kind of relationship I want her to have.

NILON. You need to take Amara to get checked out, that cough of hers don't sound good.

SAMARRA. As soon as we're done moving, I'll take care of her.

NILON. I can take her to the doctor.

SAMARRA. I think it's better if we wait though. I don't want her to keep relying on you.

NILON. You just quit your job. I can get her taken care of.

SAMARRA. No.

NILON. Didn't you say you never knew love until you met me? Were you lying when you said that?

SAMARRA. I would never lie to you. You were the first man I dated to have a legal job.

NILON. You were the prettiest woman I'd seen – and intelligent.

SAMARRA. It was instant for us.

NILON. Is it because he's younger?

SAMARRA. Please, Nilon.

NILON. What do you need from me to convince you to stay?

SAMARRA. Are you willing to take it a step further?

NILON. What does that mean? You already have everything I have to offer.

SAMARRA. A deeper commitment. A covenant.

NILON. Here we go again.

SAMARRA. Something that says we're one in the sight of God; that if any thing happens to you, they can recognize it.

NILON. I've already done that once it didn't work. None of yours have worked either so I can't believe you're suggesting it.

SAMARRA. You said yourself that I'm different. That we'd be different.

NILON. You are. And what we have works. Why does it need to change?

SAMMARA. This is a new life, new things, new goals.

NILON. What does this mean for us?

SAMARRA. We'd have to start over.

NILON. Completely?

SAMARRA. If it'll only end up here, with no commitment, then no even that.

NILON. Okay. If this is what you want. I love you, and I'm not letting you go easily.

SAMARRA. I'll keep that in mind.

Enter AMARA

AMARA. *(coughing)* Mommy, I don't feel good.

AMARA faints. SAMARRA and NILON work on giving her CPR. MEKA comes in to help and so do others.

MEKA. What can I do?

SAMARRA. Go find Joshua.

MEKA exits. SAMARRA and NILON continue to work on AMARA.

AMARA's spirit meets an angel and they dance to Jill Scott's "Hear My Cry" (Dance Optional)

Dancers start in the grocery store during song.

JOSHUA is looking at shelves for food, and others looking as well. MEKA comes in, sees JOSHUA and stops. She inches closer toward him, to get a better look. People are bumping up against each other, mostly against JOSHUA. As JOSHUA walks by her, MEKA touches the sleeve of his shirt and immediately lets go, feeling her body change. JOSHUA stops looking around the crowd and sees MEKA.

JOSHUA. You touched me.

MEKA. There are so many other people here, how do you

know?

JOSHUA *(quietly)* You stopped bleeding.

MEKA. She was right, you're a special man. Samarra asked me to find you.

JOSHUA. Why?

MEKA. Her daughter is sick.

JOSHUA. Amara?

MEKA. Say you'll come.

JOSHUA. I actually need to pass along

MEKA. If you could do this for me…

JOSHUA. I've already done enough for you

MEKA. Please.

(*beat*)

JOSHUA. I will.

MEKA. Thank you, thank you so much.

JUDGE. *(words are projected on screen)* O Almighty God, our heavenly Father, who of Thy great mercy hast promised forgiveness of sins to all them that with hearty repentance and true faith turn to Thee, have mercy upon us, have mercy upon us, pardon and deliver us from all our sins, confirm and strengthen us in all goodness, and bring us to everlasting life, through Jesus Christ our Lord. Amen.

Altogether. Almighty God, unto whom all hearts are open, all desires known, and from whom no secrets are hid; cleanse the thoughts of our hearts by the inspiration of Thy Holy Spirit, that we may perfectly love Thee, and worthily magnify Thy holy name, through Jesus Christ our Lord. Amen.

It is very meet, right, and our bounden duty that we should at all times, and in all place, give thanks unto Thee, O Lord, Holy Father, Almighty Everlasting God.

Altogether. Therefore with angels and archangels, and with all the company of heaven, we laud and magnify Thy glorious name, evermore praising Thee and saying, "Holy, Holy, Holy, Lord God of Hosts, heaven and earth are full of Thy glory. Glory be to Thee, O Lord, Most High. Amen.

Lights crossfade to NILON and SAMARRA. NEIL, LEAH enter.

LEAH. Can I see her?

NILON *(to Neil)* Why?

NEIL. She insisted. What was I to say?

SAMARRA. Leah, baby, Amara was sick. We don't want you to get what she had.

JOSHUA and MEKA enter.

LEAH. Mr. Joshua! We need you.

NILON. You. After all you've caused, how can you even…

MEKA. Nilon.

NILON. You taking his side?

MEKA. Just let us see Amara.

NILON. It's too late.

MEKA. No!

SAMARRA. Something's different about you.

MEKA. Yes. I understand you now.

SAMARRA. I'm so happy for you.

JOSHUA. Please, let me see Amara.

NEIL. You've done enough.

SAMARRA. Neil, let him go.

JOSHUA. I just want to tell your daughter to wake up.

NEIL. What kind of sick joke is this? Nilon, tell him to get out.

NILON. It's not my place to.

NEIL. Samarra.

SAMARRA. Joshua, you may see her.

NILON. She died in my arms. I know she's dead.

JOSHUA. Then you don't have faith. Amara, get up.

AMARA. *(waking up)* Mommy.

SAMARRA. *(rushing to her side)* My baby!

NILON. Truly you're something special.

NEIL. What did you give her? You planted this.

SAMARRA. Neil, just leave.

NEIL. Only if the man of the house says something. Nilon?

MEKA. Neil, please.

NEIL. Nilon, tell them I'm okay to stay.

NILON. I'm not someone in debt with you. Don't you see everything?

NEIL exits.

Everyone goes to see AMARA. They celebrate.

Dance to "Healing in His Tears" by Smokie Norful (Dance Optional)

The dancers join Jesus who has laid out the Lord's Supper. Below, we see JESUS with the disciples having the Last Supper. JESUS stands, takes the bread, and breaks it. He gives a piece to each person in their hands. He then takes the cup and passes it around. Each puts the cup to their mouths. Crossfade to JOSHUA and NILON are sitting down talking.

NILON. So what's your deal, man? You one of those extra good guys?

JOSHUA. Nothing, man.

NILON. Seriously, you heal, you talk to children. You're

unaffected by the way people treat you. And you seem to have no real business. What is it? You righteous?

JOSHUA. I'm not righteous. I'm not worthy to gather the crumbs under this table. I've been granted mercy so I work and answer to my parents. I was a lawyer, lived the best life. Represented the criminals, the loan sharks, those who actually did the crimes. Let them live to see another day. Once I represented a guy who raped and murdered a little girl – he was guilty. Got him off and then he went right out and did it to another young girl. Something in me couldn't deal with it. Like the little girl's blood was on my hands. So I started walking, left the whole world behind. While I was on the road, searching aimlessly for myself, I had a vision that I'm called for something more. That I'm chosen. Am I righteous? No. But I speak truth. I live authentically. I stay where I'm needed, then leave when my time has come to an end.

NILON. You think others should do the same?

JOSHUA. I think others should live their truth and walk in their true value.

NILON. Just like that?

JOSHUA. It's not that easy. But I learned to live by acting on the thing I am called to do.

NILON. And what is that?

MEKA enters with a foot tub and puts it in front of JOSHUA.

MEKA. I have a present for you.

JOSHUA. It's not necessary.

MEKA. I want to.

MEKA kneels down and washes his feet. SAMARRA enters.

SAMARRA. What you doing? You using my good towel.

MEKA. Showing my appreciation.

NILON (*to JOSHUA*) You tryna get that? She's washing your feet.

MEKA dries JOSHUA's feet.

NILON. It's been like twelve years for her. Twelve years.

JOSHUA. Leave her alone. I accept your gift today, Meka, since soon there won't be a chance to celebrate.

SAMARRA. Where you goin'?

JOSHUA. It's time for me to leave.

The room is silent. MEKA puts oil on his feet.

JOSHUA*(cont)*. I will return.

MEKA gets up and carries the foot tub out as NEIL reenters the room.

NEIL. Meka, baby, am I next?

MEKA. Bye, Neil.

A knock is heard on the door. OFFICERS enter the room.

NILON. What do you want officers?

NEIL. There he is, he poisoned the girl. As medical personnel, I can not under oath allow this to go.

SAMARRA. Tell them you didn't poison her.

JOSHUA stands there saying nothing. The OFFICERS search him and find the pills that were under the chair.

MEKA. Oh no.

OFFICER. You have the right to remain silent. Anything you say can and will be used against you in the court of law…

NEIL. Take him away.

SAMARRA. He didn't do anything wrong.

POLICE OFFICERS cuff JOSHUA and take him away.

NEIL.*(cont)* Meka, about that foot rub..

MEKA slaps him and walks away.

NILON. Why don't you just leave well enough alone?

NILON stars at NEIL, who leaves. Lights down.

JESUS is with the disciples in the garden. One of them kisses JESUS' cheek then he is taken away. Next we see JOSHUA being escorted into the courtroom. There is a Judge and MARIOs set up front. JESUS reenters escorted by Guards.

JOSHUA. *(to Mario)* How are you living?

MARIO looks at JOSHUA, then proceeds.

JUDGE. The State vs. Joshua Bethlehem. What are the

charges?

JOSHUA. On the night that he was betrayed…

JESUS is hit in the face by the Guards.

MARIO. Poisoning a minor

JESUS is severely whipped.

JOSHUA. He took the bread, gave thanks, brake it and gave it to the disciples.

MARIO. Possession of illegal substances,

JOSHUA. Take eat, this is my body, which is given for you.

The Guards strip him and put a red robe on him.

MARIO. Attempted murder of a minor,

JOSHUA. Do this in remembrance of me.

A crown of thorns is placed on his head, blood runs down his face.

MARIO. Obstruction of justice.

JOSHUA. Likewise, he took the cup, and when he had given thank, he gave it saying…

They Guards give him a staff, and mockingly worship him, laughing and poking fun.

MARIO. Disturbing the peace,

JOSHUA. Drink all of this, for this is my blood of the New Testament, shed for you and for many, for remission of sins.

The GUARDS beat him more.

MARIO. A refusing to cooperate with the authorities.

JOSHUA. Do this in remembrance of me.

JESUS is stripped of the red robe, and is covered in blood. He is ordered to move to the place where he will pick up his cross.

JUDGE. How do you plead?

JOSHUA. Everyone was there. You can get your answer from them.

JUDGE. Mr. Bethlehem, you must answer the question.

JOSHUA. You are not who I have to answer to.

The courtroom becomes loud. Chants of "Guilty" are heard throughout the chamber.

JUDGE.*(smacking the gravel)* Order! You leave me no choice but to put you in contempt of court for failure to comply.

MARIO. But the charges.

JUDGE. He can not be charged if he doesn't speak.

MARIO. The people want you to make a decision.

The people start to cheer.

JUDGE. Order! Put him in jail.

JOSHUA is escorted out. JESUS comes down the aisle carrying his cross. JOSHUA is now in jail. The OFFICERS are beating him. Once he can take no more, JOSHUA bends over the bed and breathes his last breath. Song "Holy God" is sung. As the song ends, JESUS is laid on the cross.

CHOIR.
HOLY, LORD GOD ALMIGHTY
SAVIOR, LORD OF ALL (REPEATED)

The crowd is still cheering. They hammer his hands and feet. A crown is placed on his head and he is hung. A spear sticks him in the side. JESUS breathes until he dies. His body is taken down and laid under a sheet.

Crossfade to a sad SAMARRA being comforted by NILON.

NILON. I'm so sorry. There was a fight at the jail. The officers couldn't stop it.

SAMARRA. Where is his body?

NILON. They buried him. He had a card on him identifying as Jewish.

SAMARRA. Jewish?

NILON. Yes. In his tradition, he must be buried by sunset. He ain't have next of kin.

SAMARRA. He changed my whole life.

NILON. Look, I want to start us over. I know we can't start where we left off, but I wanna do it like the old days. Court you right. What you think?

AMARA. *(entering)* Mommy, come please.

"He is Risen" is heard in the background. SAMARRA goes with AMARA. JOSHUA is waiting for her there.

SAMARRA. Joshua?

JOSHUA. I'm leaving. I just wanted to stop by and see you before I left.

SAMARRA. But how…

JOSHUA. I can't give you the answers.

SAMARRA. You just came. What am I going to do without you?

JOSHUA. The same thing you did before me.

SAMARRA. What if I need you? This new life thing is a little difficult.

JOSHUA. You have the ability to choose.

SAMARRA. My choices got me to where I was before you.

JOSHUA. And those same choices have you seeing yourself differently.

SAMARRA. You don't understand//

JOSHUA.//Believe me, I do.

SAMARRA. My relationship didn't get all shaken up until you.

JOSHUA. You decided you wanted more than what you're settled for.

SAMARRA. I didn't think about maybe getting a better job until you.

JOSHUA. That was a little rash, but you made new goals and started focusing on them.

SAMARRA. Joshua//

JOSHUA. We met, but you made the decision to change things around. I may have been an inspiration, but your actions are what show your faith.

SAMARRA. This is hard.

JOSHUA. The journey always is. Just do me one favor, take care of Amara.

SAMARRA. I will.

AMARA. You won't forget us will you?

JOSHUA. I am always a part of you.

JOSHUA turns to leave.

SAMARRA. Wait. Let me pray for you.

JOSHUA. You can not touch me.

SAMARRA. That's fine. Kneel with me.

Samarra, Joshua and Amara kneel

Our Father who art in heaven, hallowed be thy name. Thy kingdom come. Thy will be done on earth as it is in heaven. Give us this day our daily bread, and forgive us our trespasses, as we forgive those who trespass against us, and lead us not into temptation, but deliver us from evil.

For thine is the kingdom, and the power, and the glory, for ever and ever.

Amen.

Samarra, Joshua and Amara stand.

SAMARRA. Goodbye.

JOSHUA. Be good to Nilon. He is a good man.

JOSHUA leaves.

AMARA. Time for bed, Mommy.

SAMARRA. Yes.

SAMARRA returns to the living room. NILON stands when she arrives.

NILON. Samarra, everything alright…

SAMARRA. Shh. I'll start new with you.

NILON. Yea?

SAMARRA. Yea. But the…

NILON. Right way. You got it.

Lights crossfade to the tomb. The women come bearing their oils to purify the body. When they get there they see it is open, and they go in to find nothing. They bring out the cloths and rejoice. Lights crossfade to the jail. NEIL, MARIO, and the officers go to the jail room to find it empty.

NEIL. So this is where it all happened? I'm sure you'll need to investigate.

Documents fall from Neil's pocket.

MARIO. *(picking up documents)* What's this?

POLICE OFFICERS see the documents.

MARIO. This document certifies that Mario Smith will pay $100,000 to Neil Turken. What is this? I never signed these documents. I don't have money like this.

NEIL. That money you borrowed had to be repaid.

MARIO. With what? I'm struggling. You just got your loans waived. We all deserve to be pardoned.

POLICE OFFICER. Neil Turkens, you are under arrest for forgery and for murder. You have the right to remain silent. Anything you say, can and will be used against you in a court of law.

NEIL. How did this happen? Mario, you gotta help me out.

POLICE OFFICERS take NEIL out.

MARIO. I think you have all the help you need. Finally, I can live free.

MARIO tears up the paper and leaves the jail.

JOSHUA walks around, looks at the town, then leaves. JESUS walking back down the aisle in white. They meet in the middle, shake hands. JOSHUA leaves, JESUS goes into the town. Song "Because He Lives". When song ends, JESUS leaves the room completely.
END OF PLAY

ABOUT THE AUTHORS

AMINA S. McINTYRE is an Atlanta born playwright whose credits include: TipMyCup Productions in New York, Atlanta One Minute Play Festival, Lenoir-Rhyne University, Fort Wayne Fringe Festival, Atlanta History Museum and Working Title Playwright's Ethel Woolson Lab. Amina is a graduate of Colby College (BA), Indiana University, Bloomington (MA) and Spalding University (MFA). Amina was a 2014-15 Horizon Theatre Playwriting Apprentice and 2014-15 City of Atlanta Office of Cultural Affairs Emerging Theatre Artist of the Year. She served as the 2014-2016 Young Ambassador for Atlanta Region of the Dramatists Guild and the first Blackacre Nature Preserver Writer in Residence in 2016. She is an ordained Elder in Full Connection with the Christian Methodist Episcopal Church

PATTY MACK (*Songwriter/Music Director*) is a lifelong CME (West Side Community CME, Atlanta, GA) and got her start singing in church at St. Matthews CME (Milwaukee, WI) at the age of 3. She is a corporate entertainment producer, composer and sought after session vocalist. As creative director of several Atlanta production houses she has produced musical revues and composed original songs for Fortune 500 companies including Microsoft, Delta Airlines and AT&T. Patty has starred in several musicals across the country, performed for U.S. and foreign dignitaries and been the headline artist in numerous jazz clubs. Patty's voice has been featured in commercials for Coca Cola, GM, Lifetime's *Project Runway* and many more. Patty thanks the Lord for His blessings, grace and mercy and her family for their continuous love and support.

Made in United States
Orlando, FL
16 May 2022